Hotel Pacoima

Hotel Pacoima

Poems by

Michael Caylo-Baradi

Cover design by Shay Culligan

ISBN: 978-1-954353-33-6

Kelsay Books
502 South 1040 East, A-119
American Fork, Utah, 84003

This book is dedicated to my grandparents—

Alfonso Cainhog Caylo (1921-2005)
Librada Bugas Caylo (1921-2005)
Gorgonia Pulanco Baradi (1903-1990)
Rufo Patajo Baradi (1891-1941)

The sounds of the traffic at my back hardly impinge on what is in effect a restoration of goodwill, of joy. I do not make the mistake of ascribing this joy to any superhuman reminder of the brevity of life. I am aware once more of the force of nature. And at such moments, I experience the fullness of nature and of its promises. Life has brought me to this condition of acceptance, and at last I understand that acceptance is all. I succumb to the genius of the place, and know true felicity. The sun is God. Of the rest it is wiser not to know, or not yet to know.

—Anita Brookner, *Bay of Angels*

Acknowledgments

Across The Margin: "Hotel Pacoima," "Smooth Criminal"

BlazeVOX: "Age of Permutations," "Before Feminism"

Blue Print Review: "Cruising on Revisitation"

Bombus Press: "Prelude to a Quieter Epilogue"

Communicator: "Unveiled in Tangier"

Eastlit: "Breathing Exercises at a Dumpsite in Manila," "Prelude to a Beauty Pageant"

Eclectica: "Night Swimming," "Portrait of a Soldier"

Eunoia Review: "Marrakech," "Neighborhood Watch," "Our Island Country Wins Miss Universe Again," "Study of Falling," "2am"

Filipino American Artist Directory: "The Symptoms"

Forth: "Taggers"

Hobart: "Geraniums," "Upward Mobility"

In Sweat and Tears: "Cruising Country"

Kartika Review: "Cruising on Revisitation"

Local Nomad: "Lacustrine Dwellers"

Mannequin Envy: "Rested Somnambulist"

MiGoZine: "Prelude to a Quieter Epilogue," "The Symptoms"

MiPOesias: "Persuasions"

Otoliths: "Lombardy," "Prelude to Act I"

Poetry Pacific: "Bloom"

The Common (Online): "Towards Algiers," "Unveiled in Tangier"

The Galway Review: "Escape," "Flight Destinations"

Underground Voices: "Altar"

XCP: Streetnotes: "Alley into Los Angeles," "Mapping Los
    Angeles"

Zygote in My Coffee: "Morning After"

Many thanks to Maxine Hong Kingston, Reme Grefalda, Ian Chung,
and Gavin O'Toole for sharing their time to comment on this book:
*I am honored to be graced by the latitude and generosity of your
words.* And certainly, to the editors of journals and online venues
who gave the poems in this collection a place for public
accessibility, for the first time: Thank You.

Contents

Prelude to Act I

The room is displaced in objects begging
for his attention, a remnant of mood

and body language from the night before.
The cup on the table is a receptacle of

loose verbs encoded on lipstick resting near
the handle. Its color flirts for plans to

call her, harass her reality with invitations,
for more time together. Then, the cavalry

of adjectives about her that passed
his thoughts surprised him, as though

he is resurrecting a princess from
picture-books many years ago, and he is

the prince who saves her from a curse
that paints an affliction

in tales desperate for fairies and
godmothers to ensure a satisfying

ending. Sitting there staring at the cup,
he imagines her phone ringing

over and over again, looping back
and forth around objects

in his room, braving for the inevitable,
for whatever answer that might blow

through the fortress of charm
and a bit of wit that holds his pride

Age of Permutations

There are nights his doubts splinter into
legs in mini-skirt, with lipstick glossy as rivers in sunset.
They cup nights in coffee, stretch them in car-chases
at a multiplex, before their moons huddle
in creased bed-sheets and glasses of wine.

When not legs, nights take the shape
of hollow moons, the way leggy lips approximate
pasts that refuse remembrance. He keeps a small
museum of them, nights
of engagements and repose,

like how some images flirt into his viewfinder's line
of sight, unplanned, and become memorable
as shattered certainties.

Persuasions

Moments stretched
the night in our umbrella,

as the city levitated
countless times

in raindrops,
before they shattered

between our steps,
flooding over

rhythm that calmed
yesterdays

and premonitions
of tomorrows.

At an intersection,
the red light

glowed through
affectations

that nourish nights
like this,

pouring fragments of sky,
dripping on edges

around us, like
something familiar your eyes

couldn't squeeze out
that night

Before Feminism

He slips through her fictions
the way fish searches food, in the club's

aquarium; its ambition to grow
fins fit for oceans and myths

is as round as eyes trapped on
its head, sentenced for

diminutive freedoms
encased in dim glass-boxes.

She keeps a museum of
loose endings, charms

that parenthesize what
she must keep

away from him. Foggy
weekends of neon

device entrapments for her,
through glasses with

overlapping thumbprints.
She's the invisible

nymph hiding behind
the fake blue-corals,

waiting to be rescued, into
someone's odyssey.

Morning After

It could've been the East Bay clouds
my eyes were looking at, from the Burger King
window, dark and ready to fall.

Or it could've been the night before,
when beer and vodka mix vanished the night,
and other nights before that.

Or it could've been our conversation last
night, about how we said our words, before
the drinks drowned them,

so we could communicate better,
without the burden of phrases, sentences,
punctuations, grammar.

It's crazy how this tasteless 8am
Burger King biscuit sandwich tastes so good,
and the empty seats around me do not

feel like absence, but of a different kind,
the kind that's in my mind, that's making this
morning feels like it should.

Prelude to a Beauty Pageant

The evening glows with expectations, dressed in butterfly-sleeved ternos with a history of high-praise on this year's Fashion Week in London and Singapore, as though nights like these are flagships to promote national identity embedded in home-grown fashion. The former first-lady herself—eternal subject of contempt, derision, and satire—sits not too close from the stage, for the best vantage point in the house, where nostalgia of her pageant days will soon devour a fanfaronade of hips, hairstyles and pouty lips, all sure to delight eyes attuned to the pulse of unpredictability. Sighs of impatience raise the tone of chit-chats filled with excessive sweet-nothings, thanks to recent, successful rhinoplasties; facial and physical revisions ensure membership to an enclave in their economic class, ever convinced that the plasticity of nature is raw material for transformations, preferably by geniuses bred and honed in Makati, already gaining popularity abroad. On the row of seats reserved for judges, a hint of Igorot tribal tattoos on a man's neck leers at other men behind him discreetly. He wears the glamor of muscularity with a bald head and a beard: a paradigm of symmetry and proportion, the kind of beauty that creates a conundrum in beauty contests, against beauty revealed by the organ inside the skull. Soon, the evening's emcees grace the hall with mutual compliments about their outfits, and dimple the crowd with swirls of sporadic laughter and giggles. Indeed, the night promises to raise the stakes of elegance in the fabulous, starting with a parade of beauties from each province garbed in costumes dipped in wit and inventiveness.

Our Island Country Wins Miss Universe Again

This time, a trembling assaults us, in unison.
It's another year to forget our dysfunctions, now
levitating on the echoes of our screams. It's
like an annulment from the struggles of our
diaspora, beaming through the usual servitude
in multiple continents. For a moment, we
are an assembly of isolationists, trapped in a
bubble that feels like redemption. This
crown is not a freak accident anymore, or another
sclerotic exercise of being mere participant
in a global competition. This crown is the grace
of belief, a whisper from the God of our
rosaries, a tune we dance in the malls and YouTube
channels of our excitements. For a while, we
are not fragments in an archipelago, but a unified
vision of hope for the plight of our country,
sequined on our candidate's gown. Now listen to
the skies of our coconut trees and skyscrapers:
there's a canticle of approbation in the offing.
It's a new inflection in the cackle of our insults to
each other: we now refuse to demoralize each
other with the cheapest slang: instead, we prefer
to dress up confrontations with the glitter of
wit and whatever irony we can muster from the
conscience of our national languages. We
want to replicate our candidate's grace and composure
during the night's final question: it's an attribution
to a new age of conquest in our pulse as a people,
a hint of waking from the glum of our past. We

are not demanding startles anymore. We are forging
quivers in our eyelashes for the grand entrance of
orchids into the center of our eyes. We cannot ignore
the beauty in our backyards anymore. We gather
into a dance to anoint root systems inside us for a
new alliance, to abdicate erasures from the body of this land.

Taggers

We own the rocks and walls near Hansen Dam,
where we tell stories with our hands, as though
descendants from the void, dispersed
from sands where hieroglyphics mythicize
the minds of men.

We get there like a pack of wolves,
beyond the grasses and the trees spreading silhouettes
between the midnights of our steps, until the body replicates
a state of ease averse to light that magnifies
the contours of the face.

This is the fellowship that breathes into fraternal scripts,
astute in codes that mine the heart of roots, of hopes,
of reclamations that are never heard,
now bursting into lines, colors, cruising on
the restless rhythms of our hands.

Lacustrine Dwellers

Nostalgia brought us here, to appease
anger and loathing of previous geographies
that conquered our hearts. The calm
of Echo Park Lake floods through
polyvocal memories of castrations and
fruitions around Lake Tanganyika,
Taal Lake, and Lake Titicaca. Each day,
smiles welcome us with reluctance,
part of the feast, of an idea, of
being eternal wanderers clawed with
startling visions of beginnings,
as though standing under noctilucent
clouds above bodies of water
haunted with superstitions. The streets
offer silhouettes of remembered
lives, masks dawns must burn and
tear apart so we can start all over again,
amidst endless freeways that steer
the sun into our plans

Alley into Los Angeles

Mapped, unlabeled space, peripheral detail: my
Address' necessary, unwritten postscript, underlining
It, or my neighbors' penchant for fast-food sex,
Behind cloisters of tinted windows,

In rosaries of orgasms, furious, whispered, quick.

Branches spill from walled, adjacent lots:
Truncated gestures of a future emancipation?
Like diasporic fantasies of forgetting: abolishing
Notions of roots, being one with, of nation.

The usual glitter of broken glasses there, the
Progressive rustiness of metals, internal and external, the
Colonialism of ant diligence, inside abandoned sofas, or festive
Gluttonies on leftover food: that ancient diet of roaches.

On nights when moons are abstract or not, it channels
Breezes, breathes of snoring drunks, or operas of dog barks,
Maximized, restless, in the smokes we blow,
Fortifying our anguished laughs.

Pushing life in a grocery cart, a man walks,
Stepping on meditations. The sun shines on his anonymity,
On my empathy's poverty. After backing out into the alley,
He's in my rearview mirror as I leave for work. On the
Hollywood freeway, he's still on my rearview, fading,
Without
         disappearing,

Smothering speed, accelerating the city into layers,
mantras,
         of, capital.

Escape

I join the sound of leaves,
rubbing against

each other's geometries
in the wind.

Their pointiness resuscitates
fears and echoes

of territories only dreams
can dismember.

Indeed, trees are masters
in taking apart

moonlight, to create a
tapestry of shadows

around footsteps
begging for directions.

I must believe
in the breadcrumbs now,

spurned by tall tales
that usurped me

to pursue this journey,
where moons

transport the lost into
a landscape

of silhouettes,
where soon they might

forget their faces,
themselves,

or whatever moved them
like falling leaves

attuned to brief moments
of flight

Mapping Los Angeles

On a hill, I see its boundaries stretch,
Crawling into night-air, adjusting horizons,
Shaking fault-lines, resetting borders,
    into freeways, desire.

Its skin: a vast geography of gleaming
Shadows, resplendent textures of neon,
Immense as love in obsession,
    furious, expansive.

Its streets pulsate radiance,
Mariachi, halogen. Intersections slip into
Speed, sucking petroleum, sweaty,
    incendiary.

We are each other's maps, indulging in
Pornographies of directions, anarchies of dislocations,
Explosive, promiscuous,
    in accelerated devotions.

Altar

I see some traces of myself on-screen,
splintered into emotions with different faces,
        a theater of me, now in the minds of other

viewers and eyes, in this dark room. How are
these eyes attached to those images, large,
        saturated in color, commanding attention,

non-interactive, and self-centered? Behind the
faces and emotions up there, I see buildings,
        massive structures, glossy landmarks,

identical to other cities in other movie-shows,
spaces desperate for something to be known
        for something visual to be included in

tourist guides. The camera then takes the
emotions for a wild ride, on the road,
        to angular streets leading to a labyrinth of

bodies, shops, alleys, traffic jams, a spectacle
of movement and stasis, under a vibrant
        sun. Then the movie takes me deeper,

into scenes I do not have to believe are real, which
is nothing new, of course, just basic religion;
        you look for the spectacle that counts inside.

Flight Destinations

A hail of angels hovers on the margins of a story,
restless for the moral center of its myth.

*

The sudden disappearance of Malaysian Airlines
Flight 360 from Kuala Lumpur to Beijing
less than one-hour after take-off inspired
the most expensive search investigation in
aviation history, mostly around the Indian Ocean
flooding the world with curiosities,
conspiracy theories, and mysteries
festering in nature and the nature of
being human itself.

*

A glass of milk departs a dining table,
destined for patterns on the floor that hold
a child's delirious giggles. His tiny
fingers reach for something in the air,
perhaps for other sounds, still oblivious
of maternal patience cleaning up another mess,
another challenge testing single parenthood.

*

Words of protest scale the heights
of skyscrapers, armed with wit and fire,
before they trump on effigies that
stand for truths attuned to press the press
with accusations so egregious
one has to wonder if they're coming
from the highest office in a superpower
so suddenly unhinged from savoir-faire
against the powers of the fourth estate.

*

At the airport, your palm feels warm on mine.
But then, you're dazed and spaced out
in the firmaments of your thoughts. Later,
you left for the bathroom, close to an hour.
Indeed, the skies look better this time,
wider, despite the clouds.

Towards Algiers

The desert scatters
on our feet. It's the only

surrender that counts,
vast, unobstructed.

Winds forge directions
for us, where

suns thirst
restless salaats.

Moons huddle
a glimmering city

in your eyes.
They curve your

neck to mine,
as shadows

hold the arcs
of their light

Unveiled in Tangier

Finally, we gave in.
At least, for now.

Souks, alleys, and tunnels
guided us there,

through muezzins
flooding

the Strait of Gibraltar.
Your gestures

stretched the sun,
loud as minarets.

Floors tiled patterns,
rising on walls,

prayers, and
premonitions.

Moonlights, too,
had been squared out.

Their curves could
bind whispers,

in moments
gasping for God

Marrakech

drifts around
your tongue

littered with
souks, alleys

& nights
distilled

in silhouettes

expanding in
overlapping thumbprints

*

As always, thirst
levitates

through a garden
of hair

beyond navels
& beards

into an architecture
of curves

built for ablutions
& absolute surrender

Cruising Country

The heatwave settles on the dashboard.
We're cruising it below the eighties.
Beside us are fields of green, vast as
boredom uninterrupted. Music
from the radio takes the AC to another
level of cool. It's like 7pm dinner
without frills; the silence belongs
to the food we're taking apart. Later,
country music offers a different spin,
driving us to the edge of our tongues,
waiting for the right words to play

Hotel Pacoima

They sink into each other's arms again
and feel each other's mouth like they belong
to other mouths. Soon, a car-chase on
Netflix wanted them to drive around
and cruise the moon into another
Friday night on San Fernando Boulevard.
There are many ways of moving
inward here. There are no rules of
penetrating the deserts of a body
without family in this country.
The bedsheets are used to that. They love
the scent of whispers, acclimated in the vagaries
of love. The painting on the wall
appears to frame a city through the eyes
of fatigue and exhaustion. Perhaps
they belong to the face looking at
the window, looking away from the room,
waiting for something to happen, for
anything that feels total and immutable

Upward Mobility

First, we push the children into their games and giggles, to insulate them from obscenities circulating in the kitchen / Then we lose our temper, & act like masters of a new language for unexpected predicaments / But we cook the things we fail to complete for the day / This is how we ignore the moon / This is how we end the day / We do not reminisce / We do not light votive candles in our minds, genuflecting before an Almighty, asking for help & inspiration / We do not coalesce into restful naps & tv shows / The idea is to fortify resolve now, reconstitute the structure of ambition on the edge of our lips / This is how we survive each other's poverties, how we stew possibilities for the future / We never incriminate ourselves for murdering intransitive options / We just chew & masticate them at the dinner table, to fill the marrows of our fears

Smooth Criminal

I compose a garden party on my keyboard
every day and fill my music with souls
abducted from my neighborhood in Gary, Indiana,
years ago. Diana was a bee from our yard,
hanging out on flowers like someone pollinating
backstage doors with unusual charm.
But Billie Jean was a special case; she was
a woman who loved subtraction and
division; she was the affair every man wanted
before reducing their machismo into
something that will never happen to my
father. He was a charmer himself and
loved to chat with the biggest smile at
the grocery store down the street,
on his way home from the steel mill. I guess
she had this thing that made men
feel brand new, like my Liberian Girl.
The family talked about her accent
all the time, which made us think of Africa,
a continent so alien as the rest of
the Midwest by now since we were moving
to L.A. It was 1969. We bloomed into
garden parties in Hollywood. Then each
concert became a garden party. I
welcomed the pattern, and didn't make
much of it, until it felt like a thriller
night. Now and then, I could deceive
the demons away with a new mask. Until
a tune so pure assaults me out of nowhere,
all of a sudden. And it feels like I'm born again

Lombardy

obeys another rendezvous into familiar territory, where 10 pm bathes tiny bubbles around my son's yellow, plastic ducky. Soon, a tale expands his eyes, consumed with wonder about the frog in it. He is holding my arms tight while listening to the story, perhaps overwhelmed by the idea of a frog well-versed in human language and communication, a creature made ugly by large, bulging eyes, a squat body, and slimy skin so disgraceful and vulgar before a princess. I'm sure the tone of my voice created a female figure cloistered in narrow ideas of beauty and elegance, secured by heredity through the claws of cunning, obsessed in notions of respect and grand spectacles. Our clan has maintained the sharpness of those claws for at least two hundred years, ever alert to marry and reproduce with those who have the best pedigree of brains, physical symmetry, and social wit. These qualities are also there, in one way or another, in grandfather's inventions, to say the least, a catalog of gadgets, spare parts, and accessories for domestic living, travel, and fitness, just to name a few. They have given life to the assembly lines of mass production that often thrive on the nerves of indignant workers blistering with protestations about the state of their wages. These workers are like the tiny bubbles around ducky, unified but not unified enough and, therefore, subject to forces that would suck them down the drain, the same force that could water my family down in the future, in epic proportions, if we don't uphold the religions that continue to crucify us into an old brand of aristocracy with a commanding view into the surface of things: its duckies, bubbles, and other fragilities, floating in a tub replenishing our nakedness. I love how the breezes of Lake Iseo take over the bathroom each night, lullabying me to sleep after sips of wine from one of my family's vineyards in Australia. The lake used to comfort the bodies of my forefathers, cleansing and fortifying their memories and aspirations from the atrocities of the Roman Empire.

Geraniums

The quiet takes back the house moments after the last word. My father knows the meaning of a long shut-up to silence a screaming wife. I'm not even sure what he is after these episodes. Perhaps he is non-toxic masculinity himself. Or simply tired of his adopted country.

Now each time I feel his silence, I step out into the yard to be with the flowers. I am their new gardener. I visit my parents as often as I can. I now have a bond with their geraniums on the patio. I fertilize them with thoughts of the future, if I will have children myself, or if it's too late.

Geranium red is deep-red like blood: loud and full of spectacle, like my mother's voice. My father spends a cup of coffee with these flowers in the morning, then leaves them alone. There is enough to fish for his eyes in the backyard, as though he's going to a new place that's only his each day.

The Symptoms

are exhausting. They bleed
endless prayers.

They scar maps and ratify
calendars under

a cloud of premonitions
and superstitions.

Mirrors avoid us
for another language now:

they summon a memory
of permutations,

when night-doors longed for
bodies without names.

These days, the world breathes
through selfies deleted

over and over again. This is
how we purge dinner-time

with giggles, and reach for
the loudest laugh

we can muster. Perhaps
the hand holding me now

is a set of fingers calling me
from another universe,

as I fall deeper and deeper into
the cracks of your voice

each day, the way autumn falls
slowly from a tree,

as though gravity, indeed, is
the essence of flight

—after Jean Vengua's "Masked Figure" (2016)

Prelude to a Quieter Epilogue

The stars are fading now, against clouds sinking within my reach
They look too far to matter without the storms of your breath
These days, I cannot taste the night anymore. And mornings love
to invade me with the raging pestilence of their light

*

Somehow my shadow finds comfort in other shadows now. I'm
drenched in murmurs about the fallacies of love and longevity
You used to be my afternoons, cracking me up into colors on
the street, bursting with traffic and children looking for lucidities

*

As always, I long for the gleam of lamps on the corner: the noise
around them disrupts the sky growing darker. They set the scene
for whatever might punctuate an immensity, the kind you hold
that's cold, or something you become as you dissolve into sleep

Rested Somnambulist

On evenings, the old lady walks
on a sidewalk. Her slow steps

cover distance, a line. Often,
she cuts the line, in the middle,

through its heart. As always, there's
no bleeding. Habit has drained

all blood out. And she has
been able to sleep well, in these walks,

without bothering to close her
eyes, into the night

Study of Falling

The tears must wear
the contours of the face,
& prepare the mind
for the void. Each pore
is a question,
a memory that stings,
a voyage against
the weight of breathing.
Sun after sun descends
in a grotesque dance
of day & night
through windows,
& the clarity of water,
ready to rescue
the body from lies
& approximations deployed
in the songs of birds

Cruising on Revisitation

The car slices through my old neighborhood, pulsating
apprehension. I retrace years, habits rigid and busy as
intersections, sidewalks crowded as thoughts in

meditations. The familiar has new layers now: structures
are less structured, transforming blocks, towering over houses,
memories, how people used to move, body language

now busy on new narratives. There are more parked
cars, too, than children on the street, glossy imports, repainted,
frames modified, all shinier than innocence. Familiar

street names huddle over each other, in my car, in my
head, hiding intimate secrets, refusing to clarify
their spellings, to confuse visitors, directing them away from

the neighborhood, from the altar of pride in place: home. I
see front lawns; they visit my childhood afternoons, drafting
shadows, mothering children not to

leave the yard. Their voices enter children's ears but are
not understood. The children run, towards the street, down
the sidewalk, to their friends, to be soaked in the

summer of play, sweating giggles. I pass a boy running
towards someone, perhaps his father, an uncle, his hero. He
is running towards expectations, something greater, his

complicity with power unrestrained, understood like
unspoken cataracts. He understands religion of obedience and
kneels before it; he'd defend it like a nation and devour its

maturity like a fooled saint. After the red light, the boy is
still running, on my rearview, running from Manila to Disneyland.
He does not disappear and refuses to. There is anger

in the refusal, becoming form, resembling
power, one that builds cities,
hungry, imperial as child's needs

Night Swimming

The woods walk with
an old man, towards

late-afternoon lake.
Soon, the sun sets

on water cradled
in his hand he drinks.

Then, his body dips
in the moon-lit pond,

restful as fish,
away from banks that

sometimes lap and drown
wrinkles in his clothes

Portrait of a Soldier

He heard it,
the sound of the sun

setting, as though
its edge had

scratched the sky,
bleeding as it sinks

into the horizon,
moments

before some bullets
flew to rest in him

Breathing Exercises at a Dumpsite in Manila

5 am engulfs him with the usual hush that rides the velocity of smoke rubbing against heaps of detritus, buried over each other for decades. Time is irrelevant now, but he prefers the color of skies without the sun, a vast ceiling of things that glimmer, as though emptiness must submit to the invasiveness of punctuations. The sound of birds continues to lullaby volumes of stench, so self-assured to find new subjects to feast on. Sometimes—besides the hunt for plastic and tin cans—the silhouettes of their wings guide him to where a new find feels exciting: bags, clothing, or food recently expired, perhaps still potent with nutrients for an aging body. He often wonders how his immune system survives amidst viral mutations desperate for fresh hosts to hibernate on. As always, the past lords over the present as green, bucolic landscapes in dreams exiled from memories of family and friends. Their eyes often haunt him in decapitated heads he'd come across now and then, engorged in lacerations, ready to welcome ants and vermin for another period of gluttony. He imagines the quality of their complexion before becoming victims of psychopaths; they give him pause, often convinced that beauty once possessed their lives: a questionable quality for longevity. As the heavens resort to lighter hues again, the day submits to another commotion of young and old scavengers, now resigned to habits around these parts, quietly averse to the intrusiveness of outsiders equipped with cameras for academic and fund-raising projects. Indeed, the discovery of objects barely used or eaten offers moments of rest and satisfaction, as though something had dissolved, for once, of the unimaginable becoming tangible reality

2 am

is a trail of ants, another exodus into unchartered territory, to celebrate, once again, the body as a perennial site of struggle. They bury their mandibles into lacerations as though studying the depth of psychosis so self-assured in colonizing anatomies with the versatility of knives. Less methodical, the flies love to buzz and hover from head to toe, liver to vas deferens, feasting comprehensively on the prey at hand. Other critters worm through sockets and punctures in the body language of freedom acclimated for hunger and free will. The intrusion of drizzle presents an enigma, a kind of fiction amidst a season of heatwaves unable to regulate intimate encounters in a city of swelling sweat glands. Soon, the moon exhumes itself from a gathering of clouds, an attempt to rescue a landscape of ravines buried in silhouettes

Neighborhood Watch

The mouth is slightly opened.
Perhaps an aborted scream.
You can hear it in the eyes.
It's now a place of communion
for arthropods. Others vulture
them for a database, greedy for clues:
the liquor store throws up stories
with excessive gestures,
while grandmothers cluster
memories between ardent hallelujahs.
For now, nights can dream again
w/o distractions & sneakers dangling
from wires look like repositories
of unfettered playfulness &
optimism, instead of the usual
outrage that crowds the neighborhood like bold,
overlapping scribbles on a billboard sign

Bloom

Petals crumble without sound,
mute as constellations in a dream.
This is how winters choke
the fog, or vague perditions
in our guilt. The fulcrum
we call sky has tilted once again,
in maps that monitor
the edges of our eyes.
I like how roads accelerate
through hills and clouds,
dense as words we thread into
a dance of nights and days

About the Author

Michael Caylo-Baradi is an alumnus of The Writers' Institute at the Graduate Center (CUNY). His work has appeared in *Hobart, Kenyon Review Online, The Common (Dispatch), Eunoia Review, Eclectica, The Galway Review, Galatea Resurrects, MiGoZine, Our Own Voice, Otoliths, PopMatters, New Pages, Ink Sweat & Tears, Latin American Review of Books,* and elsewhere.

Website: mcaylo.blogspot.com

* 9 7 8 1 9 5 4 3 5 3 3 3 6 *